TOMORROW

A Plan for the British Future

by

A.K. Chesterton

The A.K. Chesterton Trust

2015

This booklet was first published in 1961.

This edition is *The A.K. Chesterton Trust Reprint Series* No. 10

Printed & Published in 2015.

ISBN: 978-0-9575403-9-2

This booklet is dedicated to the memory of Pete Taylor, Morley, West Yorkshire.

Gone but not forgotten.

Foreword to this 2015 edition

This booklet was compiled from two leading articles[1] in *Candour* in April 1961, and were reprinted in booklet format in May 1961.

The Twelfth Hour contains a remarkably honest analysis of the weaknesses - as well as the strengths - of the *Candour*-League movement. Then as now, there was a desperate need for the majority of supporters to either become more active, or to provide the funds necessary for the survival of our movement and nation.

Tomorrow is the plan on how Britain could adapt to the loss of Empire and rally around the white dominions. This idea, long dormant, and seemingly abandoned by today's establishment, has seen some interest in the media recently, and may come again should Britain escape the shackles of the European Union.

We would like to thank Jeff Carson for his help with proof reading of this booklet.

Rob Black

The A.K. Chesterton Trust
March 2015

---

[1] *Candour* # 388/389 & 390.

Foreword to the 1961 edition

This booklet originally appeared as two leading articles in consecutive issues of *Candour*, the British Views-Letter, after the Commonwealth Prime Ministers' conference of March, 1961.

The author, Mr. A. K. Chesterton, M.C., was editor of *Candour* and founder and chairman of the Policy Committee of the League of Empire Loyalists.

The object of the first article, "The Twelfth Hour", was to 'chart' both the position of the British world and the position of the *Candour*-League of Empire Loyalists movement at "the twelfth hour".

The purpose of the second article, which appeared under the heading "Tomorrow", was to define a policy for patriots to meet the prevailing situation and to offer hope for the future of the British world.

THE TWELFTH HOUR

As the hands of the clock approach twelve it becomes imperative for the Western European nations, particularly Great Britain and the British peoples beyond the seas, to take their bearings in this strange new world of the mid-twentieth century and discover precisely in what course the wind of change is driving them. Those who follow their own noses are apt to assume that wherever their noses happen to point is necessarily the royal road to the millennium — a lunatic belief at the best of times and in the present period of confusion and peril something much more than that, verging on criminal lunacy.

* * * * *

Captains of ocean-going vessels or pilots of aircraft who were indifferent to their position in space and time would very soon bring themselves and their charges to grief. Yet we allow nations, which carry all the riches of the past and all the untold promise of the future, to be navigated by coxcombs with never a thought in their heads other than to pose as men of destiny at the controls. It is truly the fact that amidst the infinitude of tasks required to keep our civilization in being nobody is responsible for plotting its course. Give any leader a big enough build-up and the assumption will be that wherever his nose points lie blue skies and summer seas. In consequence we can scarcely complain if on waking up we discover that we are about to be dashed to pieces on the rocks.

* * * * *

We speak of conditioning processes, but habit is the deadliest conditioner of them all. As long as the human mind is confronted with familiar scenes it finds difficulty in believing that anything can be seriously amiss. It even becomes habituated to speeding-up. For instance, the erection of a huge block of flats or offices may completely change a familiar aspect of our daily lives, but because we have lived with it during the course of the few months of its building we take it for granted long before it is finished and an effort of the memory is required to visualise the original scene. I suspect that the reason why inflation does not more often cause revolution is to be found in this same power of habitude to condition the human mind.

* * * * *

Because the mind so swiftly adjusts itself to physical changes, its adjustment to changes less palpable —political, cultural, spiritual, whatever they may be — need occasion no surprise. Most people are too engrossed in earning a living or otherwise passing the time to pay much heed to the changing political pattern or to note the disappearance one after another of the traditional landmarks by which earlier generations were guided. Even so, to come suddenly upon a map of the modern world must be to the more intelligent a startling experience.

* * * * *

The world into which we were born was a world ordered by Christendom, in that the Americas had been colonised by the peoples of Western Europe and in that Asia and Africa had been tamed by Western Europeans and made answerable to systems of law based upon Christian principles. There was mutual advantage in the arrangement; in return for the administrative genius, standards of hygiene, medical benefits and reserves of power with which to cope with recrudescences of barbarism in far-off lands, the metropolitan countries gained control over raw materials, spheres of interest, trading posts and strategic bases, all ministering to their strength and thereby enabling them to discharge their duty towards the vast multitudes in all lands who looked to them for protection, guidance and succour.

* * * * *

That is the world into which we were born. But it is not the world that
we now inhabit. There has been an almost total change, the full
significance of which is understood by perhaps one person in every
hundred thousand. The map of the modern world shows the nations of
Western Europe, until the last two decades the law-givers and the
torch-bearers to the greater part of mankind, precariously perched on
the edge of a continental land-mass dominated, because of the deeply
traitorous contrivances of Teheran, Yalta and Potsdam, by ruthless
Russo-Mongol tyrants implacably warring against Christendom. I use
the word "contrivance" because no other will do. The contrivance was
not the work of Christian minds.

* * * * *

The precariousness of the Western position as shown on the modern
map is vastly accentuated by another fact which the map reveals —
almost everywhere the Western European nations have been, or are
about to be, divested of control of their overseas raw materials,
colonies, spheres of influence, trading posts and strategic bases. That
they must, at the next step, be crushed into nonentity to make way for
new and evil forces would seem to be a self-evident truth, were it not
that the massed might of propaganda put out by the supplanters,
conjoined with the apparently endless capacity of the human mind to
accept without criticism whatever becomes an accomplished fact,
manages effectively to inhibit thought.

* * * * *

Lenin long ago laid down the strategy whereby Western Europe was
to be destroyed — the attack on the periphery. Readers of *Candour*
are familiar with the details of how Wall Street and Moscow, working
in double-harness, have carried out that attack at the expense of the
British, French, Dutch and Belgian Empires. In as far as there are still

a few scattered centres of resistance, however, it may be instructive to observe the enemy forces still in action.

* * * * *

Holland, denuded of the Dutch East Indies by the treachery of her allies, still holds the western part of New Guinea, but as the supplanters are very thorough, and cannot tolerate anything short of universal victory, it was to be expected that before long Indonesia would be armed and encouraged to break down this distant remnant of Dutch influence in the East. The build-up for the purpose is now said to be complete. Indonesia's "Defence Minister" declares that "decisive superiority" has been achieved, no doubt by the submarines supplied by Poland, the naval and air bases built with Soviet aid, and the huge base at Ambon built with American aid — a most beautiful *Entente Cordiale*!

* * * * *

It has all happened before, of course, this ganging up of the Wall Street and Muscovite forces: time and again the two have acted together against the citadels of Western European civilisation, to rob and denude them utterly of their overseas strength. Perhaps the most horrifying instance since Suez was the partitioning of the Middle East which presented Iraq, a British sphere of interest, as a free gift to the Soviet Union. I say "the most horrifying" because here the British Government was disclosed as being not even the victim of the plot, but rather an accessory. How otherwise explain the despatch of British troops to Jordan (as the Americans were sent to the Lebanon) instead of to Baghdad, where the rebellion was taking place and where our friends and protégés of the Hashemite Dynasty were being murdered? How otherwise explain why the British Ambassador, emerging like a hyena from the shadows before the corpses of the Iraqi Royal Family were cold, sought an instant accommodation with the murderers? How otherwise explain why the British Government took such elaborate care to ensure that the British governess at the Court, who had witnessed the massacre, was flown back in a way calculated to obviate all questioning by the Press?

* * * * *

In the same way the Macmillan-Macleod Administration takes pride in being the prime accessory to the plot for the uprooting of British interests in Africa. How unnecessary it was for the blunderingly inept Mennen Williams to declare that African independence must be at the speed desired by Africans — at the royal pleasure, in other words, of Mau Mau and the Congolese rapists! London and Brussels long ago conceded the principle. Even so, this little vignette depicting the increased arrogance of the American attitude is worth pondering over. It is taken from a *Daily Telegraph* report, which asserts that at a reception in Nairobi Mennen Williams "ignored White guests, including several Government Ministers and prominent businessmen. White Ministers and their wives were pushed aside by members of Mr. Williams's staff and told to stand elsewhere in the room, because Mr. Williams wants, to talk privately with these Africans". There is precious little consolation in the knowledge that the officials and the settlers, many of them, are receiving precisely the kind of treatment they deserve, they having been very largely the agents of their own doom.

* * * * *

The fact remains that if there was the slightest reality in the American claim to be "containing Communism", the only elements in Africa capable of maintaining order and preventing a wholesale reversion to barbarism would not be thus insulted and rendered increasingly impotent to exercise the functions from which the Africans have derived such incalculable benefits. The whole disastrous spectacle admits of no explanation other than a vast take-over bid by the Money Power and its Communist foils, presaging a new partitioning of Africa but aimed more directly at the destruction and reduction to vassalage of the metropolitan countries of Western Europe.

* * * * *

Thus it is not only at the periphery that Lenin's attack against Christendom is being pressed home. For two decades — indeed, for over four decades in one way or another — Western Europe has been under continuous assault, and now most people seem habituated to the idea that their only defence consists in relying upon an ally who uses the alliance to dominate and subdue them. They accept without question that the supreme commands shall all be in American hands. They give their consent to the merging of Fighter Command with Nato forces and will not complain when Bomber Command, at the instance of the Bow group of Conservatives who enjoy Harold Macmillan's special favour and protection, is also flung into the melting-pot of the new Fred Karno's Army.

* * * * *

In all that pertains to sovereignty we are being wiped, like a dirty mark, out of history, but as long as there is no diminution in the Macmillanite supply of washing-machines, refrigerators and television sets, it is confidently expected of the British people that they shall take no cognisance of the fact. Nor is the expectation likely to be ill-founded. Never since the world began has a nation as sturdy as were the British but half a century ago become as mentally confused — indeed, as intellectually depraved — as are the British peoples in every land at the present time. If Conservative thinking on national survival is non-existent except in times of surrender and treason, Socialist thinking of whatever school is so closely allied to gibberish that it lacks the coherence that would give it even treasonable shape. Madmen cannot betray.

* * * * *

The Brigadier from England who constituted the "Opposition" at one of my South African meetings — a man as gallant as he was dense, quite a familiar combination in professional soldiers — announced in a voice full of the strangest, most inexplicable satisfaction : "We British have become too civilised to rule over other people." As soon as I had recovered my breath I challenged his use of the word "civilised" and asked him whether he did not perhaps mean "decadent".

"I am not decadent", he almost shouted at me, as though by exculpating himself he felt that he was furnishing a clean bill of health for the entire British nation. Some days later my eye happened to alight on this passage from a London report in the *Cape Argus*: "Soccer grounds where hooligans throw bottles and stones at referees, punch players, chase linesmen and fight among themselves may have to be closed. The alternative is for clubs to build strong wire fences in front of the terraces. Sir Stanley-Rous, the F.A. secretary, admits that the increasing number of crowd incidents is causing concern and says "They happen because people are getting to dislike authority more and more. I never want to see wire fences in this country. Their introduction would be a terrible indictment of our crowds." Were these the people too civilised to rule others?

Reflecting on these frenetical mobs, and on the even windier specimens who shuffle behind skiffle-bands to Aldermaston or line up behind Fenner Brockway to demonstrate solidarity with the enemies of their country, wherever they may be; reflecting on the anti-British and anti-White bias of pretty nearly the entire British Press, and reflecting on the outright betrayal of British and White interests by successive British Governments, I wondered whether it was not my duty to seek out the Brigadier and say to him:

"Look here, old boy, you and others like you should stop being bloody fools and pretending that nothing is wrong with the British people. If you would bring to your thinking one-tenth of the robust quality you have shown on the battlefield it must become obvious to you that something is quite hellishly wrong with them. There is scarcely a single manifestation of their present-day spirit which does not stink of decay. It is the negation of patriotism to insist that to the pure of nostril the smell is really one of attar of roses. Brave deeds on the battlefield can only be derided by subsequent moral cowardice in refusing to face disquieting facts." But alas! There are so many like the Brigadier.

* * * * *

Midst all the confusions in which the British and the other Europeans are languishing there is evidence of a mind at work which is anything but confused. The attack on the Western nations at home and overseas has been carried out with an almost mathematical precision: one can almost see the lifting of the sights — after the Congo, Angola; after Tanganyika, Mozambique, and so on. Yet even when one has the opportunity of fully deploying one's argument it often happens that there are critics who admit all the facts and yet deny the evidence of design. What has happened, in their view, is the result of a fortuitous concourse of circumstances. The malignancy lies in our stars, not in our enemies, whose very existence may be disputed.

* * * * *

For the benefit of such critics — it will not take me far from the main theme — I propose to quote from a profoundly interesting *Daily Telegraph* review setting forth what had to happen before Zionist ambitions in Palestine could be fulfilled:

"For as one reads Mr. Stein's skilful narrative — and how much some professional historians could learn from this handling of a complicated story by a distinguished lawyer — one becomes aware of the quite extraordinary concatenation of events that was necessary if the British Government was publicly to commit itself to 'view with favour the establishment in Palestine of a national home for the Jewish people'.

"It was necessary that Turkey should enter the war and remain in it long enough for the collapse of her empire in Asia to be irrevocable; it was necessary that the British should still see their future with imperial eyes and regard as intolerable the establishment of French domination within striking distance of the lifeline of Suez."

"It was necessary, further, that Russia, having accepted the Sykes-Picot agreement should not be in a position to attempt to revise it in her own favour or in the interests of Orthodoxy; it was necessary that all this should come about at a time when nascent Arab nationalism had made so little progress in the area in question, and the Arabs of the Levant should have taken so little part in freeing themselves from the dominion of the Turk, that it was possible for the major Allied Powers to feel satisfied that the Arabs, as Smuts put it, largely as a result of British action came better out of the Great War than any other people '.

"But above all it was necessary that the dreams of the persecuted Jews of Eastern Europe should for this brief period coincide with the dictates of British imperial strategy as seen by such men as Lloyd George, Milner and Balfour himself."

The moral of this particular story is that all the events which were required to happen did happen. Those who argue that they happened through a series of accidents are surely rather innocent people.

* * * * *

Much the same complex of interests which inspired the earlier conspiracy is at the centre of the present conspiracy to bring about the downfall of Christendom. That is what makes it so formidable. The brains employed in remoulding the world have no peers in the science of subversion, the resources behind them are limitless and nothing, absolutely nothing, is left to chance.

* * * * *

Readers may remember that a year ago Australia's Minister of Defence Townley, perhaps mistakenly briefed, boasted to me of the rapid progress being made in preparing Eastern New Guinea for independence. When I questioned the wisdom of the step, he said: "Oh yes, I agree that we White races are cutting our own throats." When I asked why we did not stop cutting our own throats, the Minister replied glumly: "World opinion." That was intended to convey a total explanation of the lunacy. I still have not made up my mind whether the Australian Minister of Defence believes that "world opinion" — the very last thing that the planners would leave to chance is something that groweth where it listeth, or whether he knows as well as I do that it is a calculated effect of enemy propaganda. Yes, *enemy* propaganda. Mr. Townley must at least have an inkling of who the opponents of the White Australia policy are, and he cannot be so naïve as to regard them as Australia's friends.

* * * * *

As the traditional world is progressively undermined, the new world is being prepared for our habitation and it is very far from being a brave new world. The established truths and ancient codes handed down to us by our fathers have manifestly to give way to whatever shibboleths may animate the bi-sexual pantaloons who shuffle backwards and forwards to Aldermaston. National pride can command no part in the future, for Bernard Baruch has pronounced it to be "silly". That means goodbye not only to national pride, but to the very concept of nationhood. Goodbye, too, to the racial differentiation which has given such colour and diversity and richness to mankind, because that is in even worse odour than are the historic nations of Western Europe. The first chairman of the World Health

16

Organisation ridiculed the possession of a white skin and besought every Canadian couple to adopt a coloured child.

* * * * *

These are no airy-fairy abstractions. Look at the policies being pushed in every land and you will see that the devils are ceaselessly engaged in carrying out, in one form or another, their own vile doctrines. Nor is the end-result an abstraction — the One World millennium of power monopoly devised by the master-usurers of New York for their exclusive glory, although doubtless with perquisites enough for the commissars and secret police who will be called upon to run the universal prison-state. How near this evil dream is to fulfilment may be judged by the extent to which our own Western societies have been rotted by subversion and treason.

* * * * *

The capital difficulty that results from an exposure of the international Power Elite is that people begin measuring the massive might of the enemy forces. They ask themselves, and then often they ask me, whether these forces have built up such strength as to be irresistible, which is another way of asking whether the decay of the West is too widespread and deep-rooted to be excised. As the midnight hour approaches, has the point of no return been reached, making further effort futile? Readers of this journal will expect it to give only one answer and that answer it duly gives. But it is no longer an unqualified answer.

There are scattered about the world various bodies opposing the Money Power, all of them small, none of them influential. I suppose that our own *Candour*-League movement is the only serious and established organisation which refuses to compromise with internationalism in any form, and which believes that it is still possible for a revival of the British spirit to reclaim the West and save the world. In as far as we hold that view we obviously do not believe that the point of no return has been reached. But the qualification must now be stated. It is best expressed by asking the further question: "How good is our movement?"

* * * * *

General Hilton, who led a miniscule break-away from our ranks, said at his inaugural meeting that, apart from frightening Lord Hailsham, we did not appear to have achieved very much. Perhaps he was right. To have produced *Candour* week after week for seven-and-a-half years may not be a great achievement, but it certainly seems to us a passable imitation of very hard labour. So with the present writer's world-wide correspondence. Our resourceful and intrepid activists who time after time have confronted Cabinet Ministers and other politicians with charges of treason, who have demonstrated against Bulganin and Kruschev, against Makarios, against the Aldermaston shufflers, against the African seditionists, against the clerical renegades, and who have gate-crashed times without number into the world's headlines, into television and into radio, may not have achieved much, but at least they have laid the basis for achievement. The same may be said of our speakers, led by Leslie Greene, Austen Brooks and Avril Walters who have spoken and debated at universities and colleges throughout the Kingdom. If they have failed in achievement it is certainly not for want of brilliant intellectual gifts and the stoutest of hearts. All in all, I do not think General Hilton's remark became him very well. If he meant that, with our severely restricted means, we have not been able to stem an enemy advance backed by all the money and media of publicity in the world, then we thank him for the compliment of assuming that we could have stopped it and hasten to agree that so far we have failed.

* * * * *

The question remains: How good is our movement?

Obviously in my own view a segment of it is very good indeed, staunch, enduring, true. What of the rest? Even after making all allowance for the fact that men and women have to keep their jobs and maintain their families, I must confess to very real doubts. Only a fraction of one percent of our members are personally active. The odds against us being so heavy, this seems to me inequitable and sad. Do our own members become habituated to the very thing they are supposed to fight?

* * * * *

Last year it was necessary for me to make a crisis appeal for funds. Seven percent of our membership responded, some most generously and sacrificially. There are others who even today have not honoured the pledges they then made. Are such people imbued with the will to victory? And what of the 93 per cent who went their ways blind and deaf to our call?

Not only last year, but year after year I have set to work to make good the balance between Mr. R. K. Jeffery's splendid donations and what it costs to keep our movement in being. I have pleaded, I have cajoled, I have importuned, I have even placed an insupportable strain on some of my personal friendships. But no more. There are certain tasks which build up, even in the most dedicated people, a repugnance so strong that eventually it becomes impossible to discharge them. That has now happened to me in my role of beggar. I will gladly continue to lead the movement, if that be the general desire. I will gladly continue to edit *Candour* should its continued publication be made possible. I will gladly do everything in reason for the cause. But I will not again beg for it or allow *Candour* to be used for the issuing of further appeals.

* * * * *

Part of the answer to the question: "How good is our movement?" would thus seem to depend upon its ability to keep itself alive without my services as general almoner and cadger-in-chief. The logic of that answer is clear. The midnight hour is about to strike. We are palpably undergoing the supreme crisis of our Western Christian civilization. (The line-up of the jackals against South Africa at the Prime Ministers' conference was just another demonstration of the fact.) *Candour* readers know, none better, what is happening in the world. If the bulk of our members, as distinct from the ever faithful few, fail to recognise that a special, sustained effort from them is needed to match the fearful challenge of the times, then the movement will have established that it is not good enough and it will deservedly die.

* * * * *

Nowhere on the horizon is there any sign of a better movement to take its place. The idea that in this tough, remorseless fight General Hilton and the oh-so-genteel ladies of his committee could succeed where we have failed is fascinating.

But we have not failed. We need not fail. We must not fail. True, it is not possible to stop the clock striking the twelfth hour. What we can and must do is to accept its sombre clanging, not as a funeral dirge, but as a call to faith and hope and more abundant life. It must sound for us, not the Last Post but the Reveille.

* * * * *

The Reveille which awakens us from our own habitudes and frees us from the conditioning processes by which we enslave ourselves.

TOMORROW

A Plan for British Survival

When the *Candour*-League of Empire Loyalists movement was founded the British world was not as far advanced in decay as it has since become. Hence we saw our task as being in the main a duty to warn the nations comprising that world of the plot to further their decay as part of an all-out effort to destroy them. This task we have faithfully discharged to the utmost of our power. As campaigns of subversion were launched in one territory after another we sounded the alarm. We named the enemy and in so doing we denounced as traitors British politicians of all parties who betrayed their trust. Despite tactical successes, we failed to bring home to sufficient numbers of our fellow-countrymen a sense of their peril. The wolves of international finance now sweep forward to the conquest of the earth. Let those who would levy the reproach of failure at us establish that they have put into the fight one hundredth part of our own tenacity and spirit.

* * * * *

The duty to sound the alarm is as imperative today as it has been at any time in the past. But the position has now deteriorated beyond the point where a general appreciation of the facts would alone be enough to avert the doom of the British nations and the ignominious surrender of the White race. Hitherto, when taxed with not offering a more constructive approach to the problems confronting the modern world, our reply has always been that when a ship is being driven on the rocks there could not possibly be a more constructive act than to draw attention to its course and demand that the engines be thrown into reverse. That in the past has always seemed to me a complete answer to our critics, but it is no longer a complete answer, for the simple reason that awareness at the present time is likely to lead not to remedial action but to paralysis. We must, for some, continue to sound the alarm about the ship being driven on the rocks, but for others, those who have been awakened to their peril, we must use all our persuasive powers to establish that the entire ocean is not rock-strewn, and that there is a practical alternative to shipwreck.

* * * * *

What is required is not the changing of our principles and fundamental premises — Heaven knows that these have been fully justified by the cataclysm of events — but instead a re-statement of our case in terms of policy, to demonstrate that the survival of the British world is not only desirable but possible.

* * * * *

First of all we must categorically reject as institutions of the enemy all internationalist agencies which limit the sovereignty of the British nations. The enactments of Dumbarton Oaks and Bretton Woods have to be recognised for what they are — attempts to suborn the peoples of the earth and make them amenable to the will of the International Money Power, ultimately as units regulated by a World Government. In the same category must be placed the various treaty organisations which sap national independence by a system miscalled interdependence, which is demonstrably another word for dependence — the surrender over a wide area of the national will. There is no reason why treaties should not survive the treaty organisations. Alliances, despite Macmillan's false declaration to the contrary, need not be an invasion of national sovereignty. Where they do, with Macmillan's unqualified assent, invade national sovereignty, as in Nato, they are properly to be regarded not as defensive arrangements but as channels of control through which the Money Power regiments its subjects and makes the free exercise of their own wills impossible.

DESTRUCTIVE ALLY

There are some readers who have still to be convinced that the dominant Money Power is to be recognised as a supranational body operating from New York, holding absolute sway over Washington and working closely with Moscow to increase or relax world tensions as this or that policy move or financial racket may require. We have produced abundant evidence in support of our contention that such a cabal exists and that its decrees have almost the force of law in the regulation of human affairs, but for present purposes, although convinced that the Americans are as much the victims of the cabal as we are, I make no protest if sceptics read for "Money Power" the words "United States". Whether or not the United States be a free agent, nobody in his senses can deny the part it has played in destroying the Western European empires, and this it has done not in the role of declared enemy but as a declared friend — our chief ally and (save the mark!) protector.

Big Brother

Therefore, leaving damn fools to believe that the United Nations, its special agencies, and the treaty organisations are run on "democratic" lines, I can at least assume that all intelligent readers will agree that Big Brother, whether depicted as Roosevelt, Eisenhower and the ridiculous President Kennedy, or as Baruch, the Warburgs, Lehman, Frankfurter and other members of the immensely powerful Jewish cabal, has despoiled the Western European countries of their heritage and reduced them to vassalage and always, as it happens, with Muscovite approval. The pattern of relationships established by the United Nations, Nato, Seato and the rest, has placed Big Brother, whether Gentile or Jew, in the position of being, if not altogether immune from criticism, at least in a position to ride rough-shod over opposition, so that we have been betrayed and imprisoned by the very devices advertised to us as a shield to protect us from adversity — in both senses, a red shield! There can be no national independence, no survival of free peoples, until these devices are utterly renounced.

* * * * *

Secondly, and to some readers this may come as a shock, we must categorically reject, as another institution of the enemy, the internationalist agency once known as the British Commonwealth and now, to cushion its impact on the delicate sensibilities of Nehru and Nkrumah, described as "the Commonwealth". Even before the Prime Ministers' recent disastrous conference at Lancaster House, the clamour of the Afro-Asian members made this nebulous conglomeration of peoples, united by no common allegiance, an active agent in the dissolution of the British world system. Their attack on South Africa, forcing that country into the wilderness, was in direct furtherance of the integrationist policy of the Money Power, while the final communique issued by the Prime Ministers made continued support for the Commonwealth by any informed patriot impossible. This, it will be remembered, declared that the general aim should be "nothing less than the complete abolition of the means of waging any kind of war", stressed that "disarmament should be phased to ensure that no country gained any significant advantage" and demanded both "an effective means of inspection and an international police force". Here is an outright statement of the supreme objective of the international financial cabal, outlining the main structural features of the universal prison-state that is being planned for the habitation of mankind. There is no alternative in honour to a root-and-branch repudiation of a Commonwealth that turns propagandist for so vile a cause.

* * * * *

Were the internationalist agencies to be smashed — or, at any rate, were Great Britain to withdraw from them — and were the Commonwealth, not before due season, to be given decent burial, what would remain? Those easily given to panic are sure to ask the question in great perturbation and alarm. The answer is simple. Common interests would remain. In place of the treaty organisations there would be a straightforward system of alliances which neither sapped national spirit nor denied to nations their own sovereign power of decision. Great Britain, France, Holland and Belgium are all members of the Western Alliance, but no idiot could be so benighted as to suppose that their treaty organisations have helped them to give each other covering-fire in safeguarding their overseas territories: the result has been the direct opposite. Indeed, it is clear that the function of a treaty organisation is to enable the senior partner to dominate junior partners and deprive them of their capacity to protect their own interests. That is why we insist that no resurgence of the West is possible until the tyranny of supranational agencies has been overthrown.

* * * * *

What would take the place of a liquidated Commonwealth? Here again common interests suggest the answer. The countries once known as the British Dominions — the White Dominions — not only share a heritage which finds expressions in innumerable departments of life but they require the cohesion of their world system for the proper exercise of their own national sovereignty. Strategically and economically they are so placed that, once the despotic power of Wall Street finance was broken, they could, in free association, command the future.

* * * * *

Leaving on one side for the time being (but only for the time being) the republican issue, good sense would demand an honoured place in this proposed nucleus for both South Africa and Southern Ireland. The adherence to the system of the present Afro-Asian members of the Commonwealth would be on terms laid down by the White nations of

25

the British world, because these nations have been — and remain — the bulwark of civilisation in the ends of the earth and the idea of their being chivvied and harassed by the parvenu States created by High Finance in Asia and Africa is contrary to nature and repugnant to what the White race owes to its own proper dignity and pride.

* * * * *

Unlike all other proposed groupings, the grouping which I suggest is realistic in the sense that it already in some sort exists and public sentiment would be pre-disposed to welcome its sharper definition and its more vigorous functioning. What would be required above all else would be a sense of identity, a sense of common danger, a sense of common purpose. As this could only be achieved in the teeth of the mighty organs of publicity operated by the International Money Power, I am certainly not disposed to argue that the task is easy. But there is no evidence that the British people, once their wits are alerted, can be intimidated by difficulties, however great. There is much evidence to the contrary.

* * * * *

Our first concern, therefore, must be to try to secure a clarification of the issues in the minds of all British peoples, above all those who are the inhabitants of the Motherland. Our work in the United Kingdom requires an intensification of effort, but no re-statement. The issues are clear enough — treason in high places, subservience to the New York cabal, political and military integration under American auspices, the future of Kenya and the Rhodesias, the flooding of our beautiful country by hordes of coloured immigrants. But we have to do more than cope with problems which are distinctively our own. If my thesis of a resurgent world system based on the former White Dominions is valid (and if it be not valid all work within each set of national frontiers must surely prove vain), then we have also to communicate this vision of the future to our colleagues in each of the countries concerned, persuading them that only within the context of such a system can they hope to exercise their own sovereign national wills. So devastating has been the advance of internationalism and the upsurge of fifth columnism to make common cause with it, that the task of our overseas colleagues will be as tough as our own, and in Canada, because of the extent of U.S. infiltration, perhaps even tougher.

* * * * *

The last war, during which so many malignant growths were fostered, gave a great impetus to the secessionist movement in Canada. Special care seems to have been taken to indoctrinate the Canadian services. A university lecturer who attained a fairly high rank in the R.C.A.F. told me that he and his brother-officers had fully made up their minds that Canada must be swung out of the British orbit. When I asked what virtue there was in leaving the British orbit only to become more deeply enmeshed in the New York network he replied: "We'll take care of that side of it. It was, of course, an empty boast. Mackenzie King and Lester Pearson were both engaged up to their eyes in the furthering of Wall Street policies, which included a benign attitude towards the Soviet Union and the outright championship of the bogus Zionist claim to Palestine. This was the period when Canadian seamen were put into uniforms which would distinguish them from ratings of the Royal Navy and so protect them, as the Canadian people were told, from the odium of being mistaken for Britons. What odium would that be, if not the kind manufactured by Jewry for use as long as the British tried to hold some kind of a ring for the Arabs? When dispositions came to be made for the defence of North America the Jewish cabal shaping internationalist policies in New York saw to it that Great Britain, which had fostered the development of both North American nations, should be left ignominiously out on a limb. That Pearson earned the gratitude of his masters is proved by the recent Israeli award to him of its Medal for Valour! In the same way the showering of Jewish honours and enconiums on Diefenbaker makes clear that Jewish power took the change of Government in its stride. Diefenbaker's declared aim of destroying the pride of Canadians in their British ancestry and traditions reveals how brazen has become the attack on the British world.

* * * * *

Nevertheless, although Canada would seem to be the most overtly Jew-controlled of all the Queen's domains, there is no doubt that Canadians are alive to the threat to their nationhood represented by the infiltration of American capital and influence, and many of them are now prepared to reconsider their position in the light of experience. Diefenbaker ratted on his election promise to divert to Britain a substantial part of Canada's trade with the United States, but that he should have made it in the first place is clear evidence that such a move would be popular with Canadian voters. The truth is that there miraculously survives in Canada an abundance of good-will towards Great Britain, and it is not confined to men and women of British ancestry. We know many splendid Canadians of non-British origin who proudly accept the British heritage. Exacting though the task must prove, if Canadian loyalists show sufficient resolution they can still rescue their great country from subversive influences and regain and extend their national freedom within the context of a modern British world system.

* * * * *

Australia being further from New York than is Canada, the seditionists there have had a more difficult job in weaning Australians from their traditional loyalties. Even so, the attack is being successfully pressed home on many fronts and in accordance with what have become orthodox principles of subversion. The Australian Press, almost in its entirety, has gone over to the enemy. The universities might be replicas of London or Manchester or Leeds or

Cape Town or McGill. And when the time came for the cutting of military ties between Australia and Great Britain, the right man was in the right place — the present Lord Casey to do a deal with Dulles when he was Truman's ambassador-at-large and set up the Anzus treaty, Britain's exclusion from which being specifically decreed. So short is the public memory that people today suppose that the Anzus treaty is a measure to contain Communism, whereas its pretext was the guaranteeing of American protection to Australasia on the occasion of the signing of the peace treaty with Japan! Any pretext is good enough as long as it serves to weaken the British world.

* * * * *

The subversive forces are now busily engaged, as was to be expected, in undermining the White Australia policy.

Newspaper editors, university professors, teachers, civil servants, students, the inevitable clergymen are hell-bent on the destruction of Australia by throwing the country open to Asian immigration. In time the pressures exerted on Canberra will equal in ferocity the pressures exerted on Pretoria, and are unlikely to encounter the same stern opposition. If the vision of a re-formed and reinvigorated British world system here set forth is to be realized, the British peoples everywhere, at whatever cost, will have to take an unfaltering stand by Australia's side. As I see the future of the world, only peoples prepared to defend their values at whatever cost will survive as sovereign entities. In the meantime there are Australians, some of them very well informed, who offer battle to the International Money Power. They would do so much more effectively if they could divest themselves of some of the more fanatical money-reform pedants who, like most of their kind everywhere, infinitely prefer heresy-hunting to fighting the enemy.

* * * * *

New Zealand is in much the same plight. Even Government departments there take the responsibility of bidding New Zealanders embrace an Asian destiny, while ecclesiastical fifth columnists tell them the flaming lie that they have more in common with their Asian neighbours than with their British kith and kin. Auckland on a Sunday night reveals how far "integration" has gone between New Zealanders, Cook Islanders, Solomon Islanders, Fiji Islanders and the whole Pacific shooting-match at the teddy-boy level. What is now being fostered is the guiding of the same growth into the higher social strata. As in Australia, there is a certain local opposition to the Money Power, but some of it is more idiosyncratic and less stable.

* * * * *

Curiously, South Africa, although riddled by conspiracy and subjected to continued bombardment by the world's Press, is in better shape, and far more self-assured, than any other nation adhering to what remains of the British system. This is not because of any general awareness of the menace of the Money Power (outside our own League, my friend Dr. J. N. Haldeman is the only man known to me in the Union who has the knowledge, the courage, the capacity and the willingness to challenge it) but because one aspect of internationalist policy — that of racial integration — happens to conflict with the deepest instincts of the people. South African self-assurance, being based on tacit local agreement between the Whites, could well destroy itself through unjustified complacency. If White South Africa is to survive, it can only be by extending local agreement to sources of White power elsewhere. That is why the retention of the British world system and the resurgence of the British spirit should be regarded as of paramount importance by the custodians of civilization in the Union. The internationalist enemy cannot indefinitely be contained at the line of the Limpopo River unless his general strategy and design are more generally understood.

* * * * *

South African readers may spare themselves the labour of writing to inform me that the British Government is bespoke. We are not blind to realities. The fact remains that in the critical years ahead help for White South Africa is far more likely to come from the British nations than from any other quarter. South Africans would therefore be better employed in cultivating their friends than in trying (as South Africa House in London despicably tries) to appease their enemies. They should remember that a position has been reached wherein the African bridgehead established in Ghana for the attack on White civilization has been enlarged to embrace the whole of West Africa, and that a second bridgehead for subversive operations is now available in Tanganyika, where Nyerere depicts the creation of an East and Central African federation which, in his own words, "would make the South African position impossible". Indeed, even without any such federal structure the South Africans cannot hope to withstand the long continuance of Black pressures responsive to internationalist control. What is happening is war — war not only against White South Africa but against the White races. It is a war the White races cannot win unless they are prepared to fight back. One of the first signs of vitality in a resurgent British world would be an immediate alignment with the Union and an ultimatum to the rabble of "emergent States" in Africa to stop their aggression — with paratroops and mobile divisions at the ready to enforce the decree. To remain under attack with-out the will to counter-attack is to invite defeat, and what sort of a world would it be if the White nations were indeed defeated?

* * * * *

There will be those who sense danger in my proposal for the defence of Western civilisation. Of course there is danger. Danger is inherent in life. But the best safeguards against it are boldness and determination, qualities which the Western European nations have placed in the discard during the last decade and a half. What is the alternative? A rapid acceleration of policies of surrender which will make the terms of life impossible for White men and women throughout Africa and at next remove throughout Australasia, followed by the swift collapse of Christendom. If the course which I propose can be adopted before Kenya and the Rhodesias are completely returned to barbarism, so much the better. If not, then I unhesitatingly affirm the necessity for the eventual reconquest of those territories which, like the Union of South Africa, are the creations of the European genius and therefore the moral possession of their creators.

* * * * *

Once we returned to the robust attitudes which made our peoples great we should not lack for allies. The Western European nations would surely take heart from our resurgence and join with us in safeguarding civilisation throughout the world. Indeed, the American peoples themselves might be encouraged to make their second Declaration of Independence, this time of the Wall Street usurers who subvert and pervert the traditional European values and who are as great a menace to freedom in the United States as they are everywhere else.

* * * * *

I do not belittle the size of the job to be done, but I insist that the re-animation of a world system which has proved its worth, and which still in part exists, is necessarily very much easier to achieve than any of the innumerable schemes for securing the federation of nations which do not and never have accepted a common allegiance or shared the same institutions.

Mention of a common allegiance brings us back to the republican issue. We Empire Loyalists are necessarily Monarchists, and nonetheless so because the classic concept of the Monarchy as the protector of the people has ceased for the time being to be a factor in our governance. On a short-term view the issue between Monarchy and Republic is irrelevant to the South African task of holding the pass for civilization. On a long-term view it could be of cardinal importance. If I am right in my assumption that the former White Dominions, in association with a resurgent Britain, offer the only possible nucleus for White unity throughout most of the world, it follows that there must be a supreme unifying factor, and that factor, I suggest, should be the British Crown. But until we again become a proud, strong, dynamic peoples we are in no position to ask Afrikaners to resume allegiance to their former Sovereign or even to listen to our argument for the necessity of a shared loyalty. Had the British nations taken the lead in championing White leadership in Africa, republicanism in the Union would have remained a minority movement. We have nothing by way of accomplishment in this field to commend us as a nation and as a community of nations. Undefeated in war, we have now bitten the dust in peace, and defeat (my cousin Gilbert notwithstanding) knows no magic and attracts no friends.

* * * * *

The day ends for us in disgrace — a disgrace which we of the *Candour*-League movement have striven to avert. There remains tomorrow. Let us lose no instant after the striking of the midnight hour before we return to the battle and seek a decision on the issues which we have here endeavoured to clarify. Victory is for the brave of heart and the tough in spirit. In these respects we have not the pretext that our fathers left us ill-endowed.

All patriots should read

CANDOUR

The British Views-Letter

Edited by A. K. CHESTERTON

●

THE EMPIRE'S
HARDEST HITTING
WEEKLY PAPER

●

SUBSCRIPTION RATES

Per Annum (52 issues) 25s.

Per half year (26 issues) 13/-. Per Quarter (13 issues) 7/6

TRIAL SUBSCRIPTION (6 issues) 2/6 (Air Mail 4/6)

from

Candour Publishing Co., 10 Dingwall Road, Croydon, Surrey

Published by the Candour Publishing Co., 10 Dingwall Road, Croydon, Surrey and printed by the Clair Press, 111a Westbourne Grove, London, W.2.

TOMORROW

*A Plan for the
British Future*

By A. K. Chesterton

●

CANDOUR PUBLISHING COMPANY

10 Dingwall Road, Croydon, Surrey

PRICE ONE SHILLING

The front and rear cover of the 1961 first edition of this booklet.

About A.K. Chesterton

Arthur Kenneth Chesterton was born at the Luipaards Vlei gold mine, Krugersdorp, South Africa where his father was an official in 1899.

In 1915 unhappy at school in England A.K. returned to South Africa. There and without the knowledge of his parents, and having exaggerated his age by four years, he enlisted in the 5th South African Infantry.

Before his 17th birthday he had been in the thick of three battles in German East Africa. Later in the war he transferred as a commissioned officer to the Royal Fusiliers and served for the rest of the war on the Western Front being awarded the Military Cross in 1918 for conspicuous gallantry.

Between the wars A.K. first prospected for diamonds before becoming a journalist first in South Africa and then England. Alarmed at the economic chaos threatening Britain, he joined Sir Oswald Mosley in the B.U.F and became prominent in the movement. In 1938, he quarrelled with Mosley's policies and left the movement.

When the Second World War started he rejoined the army, volunteered for tropical service and went through all the hardships of the great push up from Kenya across the wilds of Jubaland through the desert of the Ogaden and into the remotest parts of Somalia. He was afterwards sent down the coast to join the Somaliland Camel Corps and intervene in the inter-tribal warfare among the Somalis.

In 1943 his health broke down and he was invalided out of the army with malaria and colitis, returning to journalism. In 1944, he became deputy editor and chief leader writer of *Truth*.

In the early 1950s A.K. established *Candour* and founded the League of Empire Loyalists which for some years made many colourful headlines in the press worldwide. He later took that organisation into The National Front, and served as its Chairman for a time.

A.K. Chesterton died in 1973.

A.K. Chesterton

About The A.K. Chesterton Trust

The A.K. Chesterton Trust was formed by Colin Todd and the late Miss. Rosine de Bounevialle in January 1996 to succeed and continue the work of the now defunct Candour Publishing Co.

The objects of the Trust are stated as follows:

"To promote and expound the principles of A.K. Chesterton which are defined as being to demonstrate the power of, and to combat the power of International Finance, and to promote the National Sovereignty of the British World."

Our aims include:

- *Maintaining and expanding the range of material relevant to A.K. Chesterton and his associates throughout his life.*

- *To preserve and keep in-print important works on British Nationalism in order to educate the current generation of our people.*

- *The maintenance and recovery of the sovereign independence of the British Peoples throughout the world.*

- *The strengthening of the spiritual and material bonds between the British Peoples throughout the world.*

- *The resurgence at home and abroad of the British spirit.*

We will raise funds by way of merchandising and donations.

We ask that our friends make provision for *The A.K. Chesterton Trust* in their will.

The A.K. Chesterton Trust has a **duty** to keep *Candour* in the ring and punching.

CANDOUR: To defend national sovereignty against the menace of international finance.

CANDOUR: To serve as a link between Britons all over the world in protest against the surrender of their world heritage.

<u>Subscribe to Candour</u>

CANDOUR SUBSCRIPTION RATES FOR 10 ISSUES.

U.K. £25.00
Europe 40 Euros.
Rest of the World £35.00.
USA $50.00.

All Airmail. Cheque's and Postal Orders, £'s Sterling only, made payable to *The A.K. Chesterton Trust*. (Others, please send cash by **secure post**, $ bills or Euro notes.)

Payment by Paypal is available. Please see our website **www.candour.org.uk** for more information.

<u>Candour Back Issues</u>

Back issues are available. 1953 to the present.

Please request our back issue catalogue by sending your name and address with two 1st class stamps to:

The A.K. Chesterton Trust, BM Candour, London, WC1N 3XX, UK

Alternatively, see our website at **www.candour.org.uk** where you can order a growing selection on-line.